THE
KINGDOM
OF
LIGHT

THE
KINGDOM
OF
DARKNESS

SPIRITUAL WAR:

That Happens Inside of You!

Light and Darkness

CONTENTS

About the Author:

I am a retired law enforcement officer (Deputy Sheriff); I served 25 years. As you know we have weapons and armor to do our jobs. We have the Law, good oral and writing skills, computer, phone, physically fit, uniform, boots, shield/badge, body camera, bulletproof vest, on the belt - radio, batons, flash light, handcuffs, handcuff key, pepper spray, stun gun, firearm, gloves, even the squad car, dash camera, radio, blue lights/siren, rubber boots, mask, extra cuffs, first aid kit, shotgun/rifle, full body gear and helmet if needed, etc. Before we are released into the streets we go through months and months of training.

We must be trained on how to use all of the equipment and weapons. Everyone must learn how to operate equipment and weapons on their own. Everyone must demonstrate that they know how to use everything to pass recruit school. I cannot begin to explain to you the extensive training even to the smallest details, for example, our boots must be shined, or there were consequences. We go through many, many scenarios to prepare and sharpen good decision-making skills. After graduating from recruit school, we are assigned to a more experienced officer Field Training Office (FTO) months before we get our own squad car. The law is designed to provide service, safety, order and peace for the community. And YES, some fail; everybody cannot do this job.
However, everyone's a winner on the battlefield for the Lord, because Jesus defeated Satan on the cross and all we have to do is believe that and walk in the word of God the TRUTH.
(I am not talking about the Military training; of course police training is no comparison to the Military, let me be clear on this).

"Thank You For Your Service"

INTRODUCTION

We had sixteen souls to be filled with the Holy Ghost in a revival. I sat and wondered if they knew what had happened to them? Do they even understand the spiritual battle they have joined? Do they understand the battle of light and darkness within themselves? I got home from service that night and I wanted to warn them of the tricks the enemy plays with our minds. My personality has always been trying to protect people. One of my worst beatdowns in the fourth grade was trying to protect someone else. No wonder I became a cop.

However, this book was created through so much personal pain in my life. We have been dealing with our oldest child who has been struggling with mental health for twenty years. On top of all of this, he has been homeless and battles drug addiction. He would call me over in the night, early in the morning. I would become a nervous wreck; my hands would start trembling and my voice would become faint; it would just take the strength of life out of me. You know the enemy planted a thought in my mind. No one is going to listen to you because you cannot help your own child or yourself.

I had become worn out, worn down, run down, tired of dealing with this and downright exhausted. It is one thing to deal with something for a year, maybe five years but twenty years. I just could not do it anymore. Everybody is saying he is grown. It is his life. These are his choices, and I would tell myself the same words too. I know all of this. I was battling with anxiety about his life and his safety. I was very quiet, sad and my family knows that is not my personality.

I could not sleep, lost my appetite, could not eat, the smell of food made me nauseated. My husband made me eat something when he ate dinner. I knew better in my spiritual knowledge, but my emotions were winning. I could not shake it! I could not help myself.

I had a dream that my husband and I went looking for our son. We found this place like a dark alley. There were people standing against the walls, people sitting slumped over and laying on the ground. Some looked like they lived there in cardboard boxes and tents everywhere. You know the smell was horrific. This was not unusual to see in a place where homeless people and addicts lived. But, what awestruck us was as we began to walk down that alley the darkness was so thick and heavy we could feel it. It was so dark that we were standing right next to each other and could not see each other. That is the only way I can explain it: those people were in such thick heavy darkness it was paralyzing as though we were moving in slow motion.

We were not afraid, go figure (perfect love cast out all fear). We began to call our son's name out. We called him by his nickname. People were moaning and groaning. We were stumbling over them because we could not see. As we stumbled up on people, we would feel their faces to see if it was our son. (As I type this my eyes are filled with tears). God's people are in such thick heavy darkness they cannot find a way out. Someone has to go get them, grab them by the hand and pull them out. That is what the LORD was showing me.

This does not mean you have to physically go get them, but you have to be willing to sacrifice yourself for their deliverance through fasting and praying. **Mark 9: 22-29 22** And ofttimes it hath cast him into the fire, and into the waters, to destroy him: but if thou canst do anything, have compassion on us, and help us. **23** Jesus said unto him, If thou canst believe, all things are possible to him that believeth. **24** And straightway the father of the child cried out, and said with tears, Lord, I believe; help thou mine unbelief. **25** When Jesus saw that the people came running together, he rebuked the foul spirit, saying unto him, Thou dumb and deaf spirit, I charge thee, come out of him, and enter no more into him.**26** And the spirit cried, and rent him sore, and came out of him: and he was as one dead; insomuch that many said, He is dead. **27** But Jesus took him by the hand, and lifted him up; and he arose. **28** And when he was come into the house, his disciples asked him privately, Why could not we cast him out?

Mark 9:29 And he said unto them, This kind can come forth by nothing, but by prayer and fasting.

I knew I had to get a hold of this attack on my mind, so I started fasting and praying. I guess I should say fasting and crying. I stopped answering my phone with strange numbers. I turned the ringer off on my phone at night. I did not have the emotional strength to do that until I started fasting. I started sleeping better at night. The Lord said to me you are not his savior, I am God. What about all of those people you stumbled overlooking for your son? They are somebody's children, and they are all my children. Oh, did I repent! I repented, over and over again for being so selfish. The Lord said nothing is too hard for me to do but you are greedy and lazy because you will not fast and pray. I have been fasting and praying at least once a week on Wednesdays for years. That is not what the Lord is saying. People of God we have got to Fast and Pray until something happens…

The Lord delivered me from anxiety and depression. Now as I continue to fast and pray; some of my family and friends have joined. We are praying for the next generations of God's Saints, the parents and deliverance of children that are struggling with mental health and addictions of all kinds. The Lord has blessed us with a team that is fasting and praying until change comes. Until our children/grandchildren and yours are saved and become Laborers in the Harvest for Jesus in these last days.

Please Join Us!

So yeah, this book came through all of this pain,
You Will Be Blessed By It!

I went to bed that night thinking about these sixteen souls that were filled with the Holy Ghost. The Lord said what are you going to do about it? I responded, "what can I do? Who am I? You know God He uses what He has already gifted us with. The LORD woke me up at about 4:00 am. I immediately got out of bed, went to my special room and began typing. The LORD downloaded The Kingdom of Light and the Kingdom of Darkness and our spiritual weapons to use. As long as we are in these human bodies, we will be battling the attacks of the Kingdom of Darkness. This is a Spiritual War that happens within our minds, and we have the victory through Jesus Christ our LORD and Savior, AMEN!

"

So then, with my law enforcement mindset and warrior mentality: The Spiritual War of the Kingdom of Darkness and the Kingdom Light that happens in my mind, makes me think about how do I come out a winner every time? I take the word of God the TRUTH and learn how to operate the spiritual weapons that are given to me to acquire abundant LIFE on earth and live with JESUS ETERNALLY.

I Peter 2:9 But ye are a chosen generation, a royal priesthood, an holy nation, a peculiar people; that ye should shew forth the praises of him who hath called you out of darkness into his marvelous light;

"WARRIORS FOR JESUS CHRIST"

<u>To EVERY LIVING HUMAN BEING</u>, You are in a spiritual war for your **SOUL, bottom line whether you believe it or not doesn't matter!** We all know that at some point this body dies and returns to dirt, but your mind lives forever and ever. That is as simple as I can make it. When you look into the mirror you see your face and body but you cannot see your thoughts, who you really are. Sounds scary uh? Everyone lives forever after death. The question is where are you going to live it?

Matthew 10:26 -28 Fear them not therefore: for there is nothing covered, that shall not be revealed; and hid, that shall not be known.27 What I tell you in darkness, that speak ye in light: and what ye hear in the ear, that preach ye upon the housetops. 28 And fear not them which kill the body, but are not able to kill the soul: but rather fear him which is able to destroy both soul and body in hell.

So, **<u>To Our New Soldiers in Christ Jesus:</u>** who have been filled with the Holy Ghost (Holy Spirit), the spirit of **LIGHT** has entered because you invited Him in. He comes in to comfort, guide, help, discipline, teach etc. that person inside of you that no one can physically see, your **SOUL.**

JOHN 16:13 Howbeit when he, the Spirit of truth, is come, he will guide you into all truth: for he shall not speak of himself; but whatsoever he shall hear, that shall he speak: and he will shew you things to come.

Acts 1:8 But ye shall receive power, after that the Holy Ghost is come upon you: and ye shall be witnesses unto me both in Jerusalem, and in all Judaea, and in Samaria, and unto the uttermost part of the earth.

Romans 8:9 But ye are not in the flesh, but in the Spirit, if so be that the Spirit of God dwell in you. Now if any man has not the Spirit of Christ, he is none of his.

Welcome My Brothers and Sisters to the Spiritual War of the **Kingdon of Darkness** and **Kingdom of Light**

"That Happens Inside of You!

If you do not know, you are in the fight for your life. In other words, where your eternal soul will live after you die and leave this natural world. I am moved with such great compassion to share some of the strat-egies of war with you. Although we are on the winning side and Satan is already defeated, through the cross of Jesus. We must arm our minds to fight. Resist the mind games Satan plays with our family, friends, emo-tions, money, health, intelligence to rob us of our peace of mind. We **no longer** have to operate in darkness, by the world's system. I am sure you have heard the saying "get all you can and can all you get." We choose to conduct business God's way, The Kingdom of Light, to be successful.

St. John 8:12
Then spake Jesus again unto them, saying, I am the light of the world: he that followeth me shall not walk in darkness, but shall have the **light of life.**

Romans 8:26-27
Likewise the Spirit also helpeth our infirmities: for we know not what we should pray for as we ought: but the Spirit itself maketh interces-sion for us with groanings which cannot be uttered. **27** And he that searcheth the hearts knoweth what is the mind of the Spirit, because he maketh intercession for the saints according to the will of God.

St. John 10:10 The thief cometh not, but for to steal, and to kill, and to destroy: I am come that they might have life, and that they might have it more abundantly. Satan tailor makes our trials and tribulations fit us perfectly. He knows more about our family history than we know. Therefore, when he comes to steal, kill and destroy.
Santan is not going to tempt you with smoking if you don't smoke. It will be something you like just for you, so **be watchful.**
<u>**He comes in ways that we will not recognize him at first.**</u>
<u>**He is cunning and crafty.**</u>

Our tests are up close and personal to us.

I thought about all of the new Warriors coming into battle after being filled with the Holy Ghost, do you really understand what you are about to encounter. Your eyes are coming open to the spirit world and the natural world at the same time. What does this mean to you? That you will begin to see living your life differently to become more of a spiritual investor of people than a natural investor of things. That this world is not our permanent home and we live this life to live again in heaven.

Romans 6:19-21 19 Lay not up for yourselves treasures upon earth, where moth and rust doth corrupt, and where thieves break through and steal: 20 But lay up for yourselves treasures in heaven, where neither moth nor rust doth corrupt, and where thieves do not break through nor steal: **21** For where your treasure is, there will your heart be also.
Yes, we are still responsible to work and take care of our business to live in this natural world but we do not compromise life in Jesus in any way.

I Timothy 5:8 But if any provide not for his own, and specially for those of his own house, he hath denied the faith, and is worse than an infidel.

"The Fight Is In Your Mind"

Why do you think we need to learn what the word of God says?
So we can speak the word of God and change our situation.
Proverb 18:21 Death and life are in the power of the tongue: and they
that love it shall eat the fruit thereof.

Or even if the situation does not change immediately we will still be able to
stand in the integrity of God. Satan tries to wear us down with cares of the
world and they are real. If we are sick in our bodies or have a child in the
streets or need money these are real situations but no matter what, nothing
should separate us from the love of God. We get rid of negative thoughts
that continue to plague in our imaginations.
Isiah 26:3 Thou wilt keep him in perfect peace, whose mind is stayed on
thee: because he trusteth in thee.

Colossians 3:1-10/12-17 If ye then be risen with Christ, seek those things
which are above, where Christ sitteth on the right hand of God. 2 Set your
affection on things above, not on things on the earth. 3 For ye are dead,
and your life is hid with Christ in God. 4 When Christ, who is our life,
shall appear, then shall ye also appear with him in glory. 5 Mortify
therefore your members which are upon the earth; fornication,
uncleanness, inordinate affection, evil concupiscence, and covetousness,
which is idolatry: 6 For which things' sake the wrath of God cometh on the
children of disobedience: 7 In the which ye also walked some time, when
ye lived in them. 8 But now ye also put off all these; anger, wrath, malice,
blasphemy, filthy communication out of your mouth.

9 Lie not one to another, seeing that ye have **put off the old man with his deeds; 10 And have put on the new man, which is renewed in knowledge after the image of him that created him:** 12 Put on therefore, as the elect of God, holy and beloved, bowels of mercies, kindness, humbleness of mind, meekness, longsuffering; 13 Forbearing one another, and forgiving one another, if any man have a quarrel against any: even as Christ forgave you, so also do ye. 14 And above all these things put on charity, which is the bond of perfectness. 15 And let the peace of God rule in your hearts, to the which also ye are called in one body; and be ye thankful. 16 Let the word of Christ dwell in you richly in all wisdom; teaching and admonishing one another in psalms and hymns and spiritual songs, singing with grace in your hearts to the Lord. 17 And whatsoever ye do in word or deed, do all in the name of the Lord Jesus, giving thanks to God and the Father by him.

II Corithians 10:3-7 3 For though we walk in the flesh, we do not war after the flesh: **4** (For the weapons of our warfare are not carnal, but mighty through God to the pulling down of strong holds;) **5** Casting down imaginations, and every high thing that exalteth itself against the knowledge of God, and bringing into captivity every thought to the obedience of Christ; **6** And having in a readiness to revenge all disobedience, when your obedience is fulfilled. **7** Do ye look on things after the outward appearance? if any man trust to himself that he is Christ's, let him of himself think this again, that, as he is Christ's, even so are we Christ's.

SATAN	WE	JESUS
IS	ARE	IS
NOT	NOT	ALIVE
DEAD	DEAD	AND
HE	WE	HE
IS	DIE	LIVES
DEFEATED!	DAILY!	FOR
		EVER!

Your Thoughts:

_____

_____

_____

_____

_____

_____

_____

_____

_____

_____

_____

_____

_____

_____

_____

_____

_____

_____

Your Thoughts:

_____

_____

_____

_____

_____

_____

_____

_____

_____

_____

_____

_____

_____

_____

_____

_____

Your Thoughts:

Your Thoughts:

_____

_____

_____

_____

_____

_____

_____

_____

_____

_____

_____

_____

_____

_____

_____

_____

Your Thoughts:

_____

_____

_____

_____

_____

_____

_____

_____

_____

_____

_____

_____

_____

_____

_____

_____

_____

_____

FIRST COMMANDMENT

MARK 12:29-30

AND JESUS ANSWERED HIM, THE FIRST OF ALL
THE COMMANDMENTS IS, HEAR, O ISRAEL; THE LORD
OUR GOD IS ONE LORD:
AND THOU SHALT LOVE THE LORD THY GOD WITH
ALL THY HEART, WITH ALL THY SOUL, AND WITH ALL
THY MIND, AND WITH ALL THY STRENGTH:
THIS IS THE FIRST COMMANDMENT.

YOU HAVE JOINED THE ELITE FAMILY OF WARRIORS FOR JESUS CHRIST

Now we operate through the Kingdom of Light. The battle for our souls becomes real and we understand it. **I Corinthians 9: 24-27 24** Know ye not that they which run in a race run all, but one receiveth the prize? So run, that ye may obtain. **25** And every man that striveth for the mastery is temperate in all things. Now they do it to obtain a corruptible crown; but we an incorruptible. **26** I therefore so run, not as uncertainly; so fight I, not as one that beateth the air: **27** But I keep under my body, and bring it into subjection: lest that by any means, when I have preached to others, I myself should be a castaway.

Discipline your lifestyle, your circle of family and friends may become very small and you HAVE to be alright with that.

Be mindful of who you hang around and attach to your life because they will have influence on you. Please do not think that you can hang around ungodly people and it will not affect you because it will slowly but surely. Sometimes we have to stop friendships because of their lifestyles. LIGHT has NOTHING to do with DARKNESS. When you turn the light on in a room darkness disappears it is just that simple. If you don't do what they do they will stop asking you to go out with them anyway and you have to be alright with it. You cannot clean up a room in the dark. You have to turn on the light to see. This is what your life in Christ does to your friends and family who do not love Jesus the way the truth and the light.

This is why Jesus said, **Matthew 12:50 For whosoever shall do the will of my Father which is in heaven, the same is my brother, and sister, and mother.**

I Corinthians 15: 33-34 Be not deceived: evil communications corrupt good manners. 34 Awake to righteousness, and sin not; forsome have not the knowledge of God: I speak this to your shame.

"WE HAVE WEAPONS TO FIGHT THIS BATTLE "

Corinthians 10:4 (For the weapons of our warfare are not carnal, but mighty through God to the pulling down of strong holds;)

The battle happens in the mind but it is over one thing **WHO WILL YOU WORSHIP**, that is the end goal. I was talking to a new convert, a young lady. She had recently received the Holy Ghost. So we were discussing the Kingdom of Darkness and the Kingdom of Light. The young lady was basically saying that because I have more experience in trials and tribulation that it is easier for me to live a holy lifestyle. She went on to say that she is new to this and in her ignorance she would make many more mistakes.
She said, I am young and still want to do certain things and that I did not understand her struggle. My response to her was that everybody has struggles in this life walking with God are not walking with him. Our struggles are made just for us no matter what age. The struggles do not go away or get easier, we just choose the way of the Kingdom of Light.

"The greatest gift is our freedom to choose who we want to follow."

The struggle in between is all the **Stuff You Like** to put in your salad. If one hundred people made their own salad and there were one hundred different food items to choose from, no two people, I mean no two people would have the exact same salad, but the end goal is everybody would have their salad, fixed just like they like it.

So then, Satan knows what we like even though we don't know. Satan knows our weaknesses because he knows our parents , grandparents, great grand etc. their weaknesses. He knows more about our family history than we know. Therefore, he tailor designs our trials and tribulations just for us, just **like we put stuff** in our own salad. However, all the in between stuffing of trials we go through is the **fight for our souls (mind)**.

You know people can experience the same trial but how it affects them can be totally different; because no two people are the same. The end goal is still our soul. Our battle is to choose the Kingdom of Light to follow in Jesus' path according to the word of God. If we choose vengeance against someone that is the Kingdom of Darkness operating in us. Vengeance is mine saith the Lord; is the Kingdom of Light

Ephesians 6:10-17 Finally, my brethren, be strong in the Lord, and in the power of his might. 11 Put on the whole armour of God, that ye may be able to stand against the wiles of the devil. 12 For we wrestle not against flesh and blood, but against principalities, against powers, against the rulers of the darkness of this world, against spiritual wickedness in high places.

13 Wherefore take unto you the whole armour of God, that ye may be able to withstand in the evil day, and having done all, to stand. 14 Stand therefore, having your loins girt about with truth, and having on the breastplate of righteousness; 15 And your feet shod with the preparation of the gospel of peace; 16 Above all, taking the shield of faith, wherewith ye shall be able to quench all the fiery darts of the wicked. 17 And take the helmet of salvation, and the sword of the Spirit, which is the word of God.

Your Thoughts:

Your Thoughts:

Your Thoughts:

_____

_____

_____

_____

_____

_____

_____

_____

_____

_____

_____

_____

_____

_____

_____

_____

_____

_____

Your Thoughts:

THE WORD OF GOD

(Bible) is the TRUTH and the LIGHT, nothing that we think, feel or see supersedes the word of God, things present or things to come. God's word must be the infallible and immutable TRUTH in your life. We must be fully persuaded and confident in our minds that the plan of salvation through Jesus Christ is the one and only true gospel to get to heaven. Jesus was born by a virgin, lived a perfect life without sin, died on the cross, rose from the dead with all power in heaven and on earth. Jesus is our only savior, mediator, Lord of Lords and King of Kings. **ROMANS 8:34 Who is he that condemneth? It is Christ that died, yea rather, that is risen again, who is even at the right hand of God, who al-so maketh intercession for us.** THIS IS THE HELMET OF SALVATION and **THE SWORD OF THE SPIRIT WHICH IS THE WORD OF GOD, We must know the word of God for ourselves and be willing unto death to live by it. We fight the Kingdom of Darkness with the word of God - pray-ing the word, speaking the word, witnessing the word and living the word. The word of God becomes alive in us as we obey it. Standing for the truth and standing in the truth. The war is constantly going on in your mind to make you doubt God's word in some way. In other words, your loins girded about with truth is your back wrapped tight and genitals protected. You can stand up straight with a good strong back. The truth makes you stand tall and confident. Protecting your genitals protects your children and gen-erations to come that you will teach them the truth - God's Word and they will carry on in it.**

Matthew 4:4
But he answered and said, it is written, Man shall not live by bread alone, but by every word that proceedeth out of the mouth of God.

Mark 13:31

Heaven and earth shall pass away: but my words shall not pass away.

"The WORD of GOD MUST RULE OVER EVERYTHING"

The Word of God!

The Word of God!   The Word of God!

KNOW IT!

BELIEVE IT!

SPEAK IT!

SPEAK IT!

SPEAK IT!

The Word Of God:

_____

_____

_____

_____

_____

_____

_____

_____

_____

_____

_____

_____

_____

_____

_____

_____

_____

_____

_____

_____

FAITH SPEAKS

The shield of faith is all of the things that God has already brought you through. Your past experiences tell to you that he will bring you through this one and the next one and so on, because he has never failed. **Psalms 30:5** Every word of God is pure: he is a shield unto them that put their trust in him. You can quench the fiery darts of the wicked because you will remind yourself of the past victories over the devil and those thoughts of doubt and defeat will leave your mind and you will rejoice in victory, before you receive it.

Hebrews 11:1 Now faith is the substance of things hoped for, the evidence of things not seen. Faith - to remember proven experience of other things that God has already brought me through are substances. Now I believe in God for this and things to come, faith grows and grows. Without faith it is impossible to please God. You must believe in God's word to change you and to change situations in life, period.

Hebrews 11:6 But without faith it is impossible to please him: for he that cometh to God must believe that he is, and that he is a rewarder of them that diligently seek him. If you told your child something that you were going to do for them and he/she responded, I don't believe you Dad/Mom. How would that make you feel? Then, how do you think God feels if we are praying for something but down in your heart you do not believe he is going to do it. On the other hand, if your child responds to Dad/Mom I am so excited! I can't wait! That is exactly what God wants us to get excited about what you are asking because you know he is going to do it, according to his will.

Romans 10:17 So then faith cometh by hearing, and hearing by the word of God. Remember faith comes by hearing, and hearing, and hearing. We never stop growing in faith. **Romans 12:3** For I say, through the grace given unto me, to every man that is among you, not to think of himself more highly than he ought to think; but to think soberly, according as God hath dealt to every man the measure of faith.

Mark 11:22 And Jesus answering saith unto them, Have faith in God. 23 For verily I say unto you, that whosoever shall say unto this mountain, Be thou removed, and be thou cast into the sea; and shall not doubt in his heart, but shall believe that those things which he saith shall come to pass; he shall have whatsoever he saith.

As God continues to answer our prayers our faith and confidence continues to increase more and more and more in believing His word. If you were sick with cancer and the doctor said OK, you are going to need Chemotherapy, radiation then surgery. This process should give you a 90% chance of getting rid of cancer. Stay away from negative talkers. I knew somebody that had the same thing and they died, you don't need to hear that. Surround yourself with believers. You are going to do what the doctor says because you believe him. However, you have to go through the process which takes time, effort, and some suffering and if it works you will have faith in that doctor. You will even tell others about him. If you break your leg you are going to have to wear a brace for some weeks and afterwards physical therapy. Your leg will not heal overnight, and physical therapy may hurt but it will build strength. I need you to understand the process of building your faith in God. Even with a cold, flu, or corona virus you have to take medicine, maybe prescription meds, drink plenty of fluids, stay in the bed, and stay away from others over a period of time to feel better or get well. I say this because reading, studying, speaking the scriptures over and over and listening to the preached word of God over and over builds your faith. It is a process.

FAITH comes by hearing and hearing and hearing and hearing…

"CHANGE YOUR

RANGE

TO

STRANGE"

SPEAK INTO EXISTENCE!

MATTHEW 16:19 And I will give unto thee the keys of the kingdom of heaven: and whatsoever thou shalt bind on earth shall be bound in heaven: and whatsoever thou shalt loose on earth shall be loosed in heaven.

FAITH:

Your Thoughts:

_____

_____

_____

_____

_____

_____

_____

_____

_____

_____

_____

_____

_____

_____

_____

_____

Your Thoughts:

Your Thoughts:

_____

_____

_____

_____

_____

_____

_____

_____

_____

_____

_____

_____

_____

_____

_____

_____

_____

_____

_____

Your Thoughts:

_____
_____
_____
_____
_____
_____
_____
_____
_____
_____
_____
_____
_____
_____
_____
_____
_____
_____

PRAYER

You must pray but what good is prayer if you do not believe that you are going to get what you ask for, this is why faith is so important. In the prayer that Jesus taught the disciples first start with Reverence of who God is our Father, where God is in heaven and God's Holy Name above everyone and everything. Jesus clarifies that we are praying to the source of life itself - Worship who God is in his Glory, Majesty and Power. The second section of the prayer we acknowledge our dependance on God for everything and **give us** daily bread, **forgive us, lead us** and **deliver us.** Food represents our daily physical needs such as shelter, clothes etc., forgiveness - what we have done and what others have done to us let it go, to lead us and deliverance represents we need Him in this spiritual war we are in. The closing section of prayer Reverence, worships and glorifies God to the highest in all his Glorious Splendor.

Pray for others! No matter what is going on in our lives we should always pray for others and the Lord will answer our prayers and bless us. **Job 42:10** And the LORD turned the captivity of Job, when he prayed for his friends: also, the LORD gave Job twice as much as he had before.

Matthew 11:24 Therefore I say unto you, What things soever ye desire, when ye pray, believe that ye receive them, and ye shall have them. **Romans 6:8-18 8** Be not ye therefore like unto them: for your Father knoweth what things ye have need of, before ye ask him. **9** After this manner therefore pray ye: Our Father which art in heaven, Hallowed be thy name.

10 Thy kingdom come, Thy will be done on earth, as it is in heaven. **11** Give us this day our daily bread. **12** And forgive us our debts, as we forgive our debtors. **13** And lead us not into temptation, but deliver us from evil: For thine is the kingdom, and the power, and the glory, forever. Amen.

14 For if ye forgive men their trespasses, your heavenly Father will also forgive you: **15** But if ye forgive not men their trespasses, neither will your Father forgive your trespasses. **16** Moreover when ye fast, be not, as the hypocrites, of a sad countenance: for they disfigure their faces, that they may appear unto men to fast. Verily I say unto you, They have their reward. **17** But thou, when thou fastest, anoint thine head, and wash thy face; **18** That thou appear not unto men to fast, but unto thy Father which is in secret: and thy Father, which seeth in secret, shall reward thee openly.

SPEAK

WAIT

LISTEN

OBEY

PRAYER:

Your Thoughts:

_____

_____

_____

_____

_____

_____

_____

_____

_____

_____

_____

_____

_____

_____

_____

_____

_____

_____

Your Thoughts:

Your Thoughts:

Your Thoughts:

FORGIVE

We must forgive, or we will not be forgiven of anything we have done whether we are aware of it or not. In other words, you are wasting your time praying for something if you have unforgiveness in your heart because God will not forgive you.

Mark 11:25 And when ye stand praying, forgive, if ye have ought against any: that your Father also which is in heaven may forgive you your trespasses. 26 But if ye do not forgive, neither will your Father which is in heaven forgive your trespasses.

LUKE 6:27-28 But I say unto you which hear, Love your enemies, do good to them which hate you, 28 Bless them that curse you, and pray for them which despitefully use you.

KINGDOM OF LIGHT

Just because you have been rejected does not mean you have to live a life of rejection. Pray for those who have hurt you, I mean pray for them until you mean it! God will heal your broken heart and make you whole.

FORGIVE:

Your Thoughts:

Your Thoughts:

_____

_____

_____

_____

_____

_____

_____

_____

_____

_____

_____

_____

_____

_____

_____

_____

_____

Your Thoughts:

Your Thoughts:

LOVE

Even after we have done all of the right things, we must love our neighbor; the second commandment from God. The first Commandment love the Lord with all of our heart, mind, soul and strength. When we love God with all of our emotions, intellect, desires and physical and mental coping. Therefore, you cannot love God and not love his people, humanity. **So, for some reason we seem to think that we can love God and hate someone "that is impossible."**

I Corinthians 13:1-8 Though I speak with the tongues of men and of angels, and have not charity, I am become as sounding brass, or a tinkling cymbal. **2** And though I have the gift of prophecy, and understand all mysteries, and all knowledge; and though I have all faith, so that I could remove mountains, and have not charity, I am nothing. **3** And though I bestow all my goods to feed the poor, and though I give my body to be burned, and have not charity, it profiteth me nothing. **4** Charity suffereth long, and is kind; charity envieth not; charity vaunteth not itself, is not puffed up, **5** Doth not behave itself unseemly, seeketh not her own, is not easily provoked, thinketh no evil; **6** Rejoiceth not in iniquity, but rejoiceth in the truth; **7** Beareth all things, believeth all things, hopeth all things, endureth all things. **8** Charity never faileth: but whether there be prophecies, they shall fail; whether there be tongues, they shall cease; whether there be knowledge, it shall vanish away.

Matthew 5:43-48 Ye have heard that it hath been said, Thou shalt love thy neighbour, and hate thine enemy. **44** But I say unto you, Love your enemies, bless them that curse you, do good to them that hate you, and pray for them which despitefully use you, and persecute you; **45** That ye may be the children of your Father which is in heaven: for he maketh his sun to rise on the evil and on the good, and sendeth rain on the just and on the unjust.

" LOVE THE KINGDOM OF LIGHT "

" THEN YOU WILL LOVE THE TRUTH "

Romans 12:2
And be not conformed to this world: but be ye transformed by the renewing of your mind, that ye may prove what is that good, and acceptable, and perfect, will of God.

LOVE:

Your Thoughts:

_____
_____
_____
_____
_____
_____
_____
_____
_____
_____
_____
_____
_____
_____
_____
_____
_____
_____

Your Thoughts:

_____

_____

_____

_____

_____

_____

_____

_____

_____

_____

_____

_____

_____

_____

_____

_____

_____

_____

Your Thoughts:

Your Thoughts:

WORSHIP

John 4:23 Yet a time is coming and has now come when the true worshipers will worship the Father in the Spirit and in truth, for they are the kind of worshipers the Father seeks. When everything in your life seems as though it is falling about, just begin to worship God and tell him how wonderful he is. No matter what is going on in our lives we worship God because he is just that our God and we trust him in every situation.

Ephesians 5:9 speaking to one another with psalms, hymns, and songs from the Spirit. Sing and make music from your heart to the Lord, **Colossians 3:6** Let the message of Christ dwell among you richly as you teach and admonish one another with all wisdom through psalms, hymns, and songs from the Spirit, singing to God with gratitude in your hearts.

Acts 16: 25-34 About midnight Paul and Silas were praying and singing hymns to God, and the other prisoners were listening to them.
26 Suddenly there was such a violent earthquake that the foundations of the prison were shaken. At once all the prison doors flew open, and everyone's chains came loose. **27** The jailer woke up, and when he saw the prison doors open, he drew his sword and was about to kill himself because he thought the prisoners had escaped. **28** But Paul shouted, "Don't harm yourself! We are all here!" **29** The jailer called for lights, rushed in and fell trembling before Paul and Silas. **30** He then brought them out and asked, "Sirs, what must I do to be saved?" **31** They replied, "Believe in the Lord Jesus, and you will be saved—you and your household." **32** Then they spoke the word of the Lord to him and to all the Bothers in his house. **33** At that hour of the night the jailer took them and washed their wounds; then immediately he and all his household were baptized. **34** The jailer brought them into his house and set a meal before them; he was filled with joy because he had come to believe in God—he and his whole household.

Miracles happen when we worship God in our roughest, toughest, hardest trials because God is being Glorified - Period.

"WHEN WE WORSHIP"

WAr-ShIP hAPPEns

WORSHIP:

Your Thoughts:

_____

_____

_____

_____

_____

_____

_____

_____

_____

_____

_____

_____

_____

_____

_____

Your Thoughts:

_____

_____

_____

_____

_____

_____

_____

_____

_____

_____

_____

_____

_____

_____

_____

_____

_____

_____

Your Thoughts:

Your Thoughts:

_____
_____
_____
_____
_____
_____
_____
_____
_____
_____
_____
_____
_____
_____
_____
_____
_____
_____
_____

SANCTIFICATION

The breastplate of righteousness protects your thoughts by being aware of what you say, watch on tv/social media, listen to on the radio/social media, eat, drink and the company you keep. I was fall-ing asleep and my husband was watching this gangster movie. I dreamed that night that one of my nieces was selling drugs and robbing gangsters. She doesn't live that type of lifestyle, though. However, what I am saying is the Kingdom of Darkness can come in your life through any door we open. I do not watch scary mov-ies, they just make me anxious and I don't like that feeling. Protect yourself from opening opportunities for the Kingdom of Darkness to enter your thoughts, even your sub-conscience. Whatever those weaknesses are in your life, close that door. Even if you fail, repent every day and continue to follow Jesus. The word of God washes you clean by practicing doing it everyday. Everything we do, it must be to glorify him and him alone. Our motives should always be to the will of God through Jesus Christ according to his word.

Deny yourself, when you want something or want to do something you should not do, - you tell yourself NO!
Love, forgiving, obeying, giving, integrity, being sober all of these weapons come under the breastplate of righteousness.

2 Corinthians 7:1 Having therefore these promises, dearly beloved, let us cleanse ourselves from all filthiness of the flesh and spirit, perfecting holiness in the fear of God.

I Corinthians 15: 31 I protest by your rejoicing which I have in Christ Jesus our Lord, I die daily. I die daily means - I daily constantly and consistently make choices based on what the word of God says I should do. Even when I fail in doing those things I get up the next day with the same mind to obey the word of God without trying to justify or modify it to fit what I desire to do.

Romans 2:29 But he is a Jew, which is one inwardly; and circumcision is that of the heart, in the spirit, and not in the letter; whose praise is not of men, but of God.

Matthew 13-23 13 Enter ye in at the strait gate: for wide is the gate, and broad is the way, that leadeth to destruction, and many there be which go in thereat: **14** Because strait is the gate, and narrow is the way, which leadeth unto life, and few there be that find it. **15** Beware of false prophets, which come to you in sheep's clothing, but inwardly they are ravening wolves. **16** Ye shall know them by their fruits. Do men gather grapes of thorns, or figs of thistles? **17** Even so every good tree bringeth forth good fruit; but a corrupt tree bringeth forth evil fruit. **18** A good tree cannot bring forth evil fruit, neither can a corrupt tree bring forth good fruit. **19** Every tree that bringeth not forth good fruit is hewn down, and cast into the fire. **20** Wherefore by their fruits ye shall know them. **21** Not every one that saith unto me, Lord, Lord, shall enter into the kingdom of heaven; but he that doeth the will of my Father which is in heaven. **22** Many will say to me in that day, Lord, Lord, have we not prophesied in thy name? and in thy name have cast out devils? and in thy name done many wonderful works? **23** And then will I profess unto them, I never knew you: depart from me, ye that work iniquity. No matter what the preacher, prophet, pastor etc. is saying, what are they doing? What kind of people follow them? Where do they go? Who do they socialize with outside of church? Sometimes it is difficult to know. However, you are responsible to do your own due diligence and do not follow anyone blindly. We do not want another Jim Jones situation. Our works alone are not sanctification, motives of the heart are **what moves GOD!** Why you do what you do. We do not want our works for God to be rejected and burned in judgment. **Hebrews 4:12** For the word of God is quick and powerful, and sharper than any two-edged sword, piercing even to the dividing asunder of soul and spirit, and of the joints and marrow, and is a discerner of the thoughts and intents of the heart.
(Check Your Motives, we cannot fool God)

SANCTIFICATION:

OBEDIENT

We must be willing to do whatever the word of God say. The mem-bers of God's Family dedicate our lives doing the will of our Fa-ther. Therefore, it is his will to be done! This is not, have it your way **God does not spoil children!** Everyone must be obedient to the Word of God no exceptions. If we hear the word of God and refuse to obey it. Over time we will not remember who we are suppose be. Each day of willful disobe-dience over a long period of time, will CHANGE us. We will not recognize ourselves over the years, we will not know who we are - from looking at what we are doing.

Self deception is the worst kind, the lies you tell yourself and believe them, PRIDE!

James 1:22-24 22 But be ye doers of the word, and not hearers only, deceiving your own selves. **23** For if any be a hearer of the word, and not a doer, he is like unto a man beholding his natural face in a glass: **24** For he beholdeth himself, and goeth his way, and straightway forgetteth what manner of man he was.

I Samuel 15:22 And Samuel said, Hath the LORD as great delight in burnt offerings and sacrifices, as in obeying the voice of the LORD? Behold, to obey is better than sacrifice, and to hearken than the fat of rams. Obedience is better than sacrifice. We heard this many times growing up. I think we all can relate to this. Doing what is asked of you is better than giving me presents after you have done what you wanted to do. You are basically disrespecting my wishes and saying I do not care about what you want or how you feel about it. What good are presents if I do not want them? I just want you to do what I asked you to do.This proves to me you really care about me. Simple ugh?

Exodus 20:6 but showing love to a thousand generations of those who love me and keep my commandments.

Luke 9:23 And he said to them all, If any man will come after me, let him deny himself, and take up his cross daily, and follow me. Hebrews 13:17 Obey them that have the rule over you, and submit yourselves: for they watch for your souls, as they that must give account, that they may do it with joy, and not with grief: for that is unprofitable for you. Psalms 20:2 Send thee help from the sanctuary, and strengthen thee out of Zion;

OH - BE - YES

OBEYS

OBEDIENT:

Your Thoughts:

Your Thoughts:

Your Thoughts:

_____

_____

_____

_____

_____

_____

_____

_____

_____

_____

_____

_____

_____

_____

_____

_____

Your Thoughts:

BE SOBER

I Peter 5:8 Be sober, be vigilant; because your adversary the devil, as a roaring lion, walketh about, seeking whom he may devour: No, Soldier in battle can fight at his best if he is not sober. You must be sharp mentally and physically fit for combat. Critical thinking up strategies of engagement as the battle evolves, also to be able to communicate clearly and concisely and ready for combat or fast on your feet, running, shooting and fighting. Now, if you are under the influence of any type of drugs or alcohol you will become a casualty of war and you may cost your fellow soldiers some of their lives because they are depending on you to have their backs. Speak the word of God just like Jesus did when the devil came to him. Jesus said, man cannot live by bread alone but by every word that proceeds out of the month of God.

We must be at our best because when the Kingdom of darkness comes against our mind we must be able to resist him. The battle starts in the mind if the devil can get our imagination filled with fear, doubt, defeat, insecurity, manipulation, depression, anxiety, confusion, anger, revenge, hopelessness, suicide, loneliness, etc., and we begin to believe him.

Then everything else will follow,eventually the negative thoughts will cause a chain reaction of negative behavior. You must never believe the worst in life be-cause Jesus came to give us life and life more abundantly. This is why we must be sober to meditate on the word of God, speak the word of God over our life, family and friends.

Therefore, when our thoughts are cluttered with negativity that is an attack from the Kingdom of darkness. That is Satan coming to kill, steal and destroy. The devil would like for us to think our problem is our brothers and sisters but he is our enemy, the devil. We must stay Sober Mind!

Our Greatest Battles To Win Are Within!

II Thessalonians 2:10 And with all deceivableness of unrighteousness in them that perish; because they received not the **love of the truth,** that they might be saved. You must love the truth and work to-ward obeying it when you hear it, no matter how you feel or think about it. The word of God has the final say so in your life. If you think that God is asking you to do something you cannot do, ask him to help you and he will. On the contrary, do not say God's word is not true just because you struggle with believing it. To love God is to love his word which is the truth and this is the light of life. Remember the Kingdom of Darkness and The Kingdom of Light both want your soul and you must choose.
We make these choices deliberately everyday.

Philippians 4:4-9 4 Rejoice in the Lord always: and again I say, Rejoice. 5 Let your moderation be known unto all men. The Lord is at hand. 6 Be careful for nothing; but in every thing by prayer and supplication with thanksgiving let your requests be made known unto God. 7 And the peace of God, which passeth all understanding, shall keep your hearts and minds through Christ Jesus. 8 Finally, brethren, whatsoever things are true, whatsoever things are honest, whatsoever things are just, whatsoever things are pure, whatsoever things are lovely, whatsoever things are of good report; if there be any virtue, and if there be any praise, think on these things. 9 Those things, which ye have both learned, and received, and heard, and seen in me, do: and the God of peace shall be with you.

II Timothy 1:7 For God hath not given us the spirit of fear; but of power, and of love, and of a sound mind. We must not and cannot be afraid to stand in the power of TRUTH God's Word and in love **knowing in our hearts** that it is just right to do. You know society today likes to modify. I must say cell phones and microwaves are wonderful modifications.

However, the word of God cannot be modified to fit our lifestyle.

Since Marijuana (drugs) has been legalized in some states people tend to think that it is alright with God. I tell you the word of God supersedes any man made law. Anything that alters your cognitive ability when you ingest, inhale or inject is a drug. The Holy Ghost is our comforter. Not only that depression and anxiety alters your cognitive thinking. If you cannot get out of the bed, go to work, take care of your children and just do day to day responsibilities because of depression/anxiety the spirit of darkness has captured your thinking and emotions **John 14:26** But the Comforter, which is the Holy Ghost, whom the Father will send in my name, he shall teach you all things, and bring all things to your remembrance, whatsoever I have said unto you. There are **NO gray** areas in this fight over your soul. **The Kingdom of Darkness OR the Kingdom of Light!** God does not leave room to justify us continuing… to commit sinful acts. We must repent and change. **We do not use drugs, alcohol, greed, perversion, secular music, witchcraft, partying, elicit sex, anything of darkness to escape, comfort and cope with our problems.**

"YOU MUST BE SOLD OUT - ALL THE WAY OUT, JESUS IS OUR ONE AND ONLY SOURCE of LIFE and LIFE MORE ABUNDANTLY."

II Corinthians 1:3-4

Blessed be God, even the Father of our Lord Jesus Christ, the Father of mercies, and the God of all comfort; 4 Who comforteth us in all our tribulation, that we may be able to comfort them which are in any trouble, by the comfort wherewith we ourselves are comforted of God.

31

I AM MY BROTHER'S KEEPER!

BE SOBER

=

BE BROES

BE SOBER:

Your Thoughts:

Your Thoughts:

Your Thoughts:

Your Thoughts:

_____

_____

_____

_____

_____

_____

_____

_____

_____

_____

_____

_____

_____

_____

_____

_____

_____

_____

_____

INTEGRITY

You know it is like we don't talk about integrity enough in the church. For some reason we know we should do it but it is a sore spot for some people of God. However, we should practice saying what is right, thinking what is right, doing what right **when no one even knows.** I know sometimes even as people of God it is very difficult to get along with others family, friends, co-workers, and even our brothers and sisters in the Lord.
Let your integrity speak for your character.

Psalms 7-10 My defense is of God, which saveth the upright in heart.

Romans 8-21 8 Or he that exhorteth, on exhortation: he that giveth, let him do it with simplicity; he that ruleth, with diligence; he that sheweth mercy, with cheerfulness. **9** Let love be without dissimulation. Abhor that which is evil; cleave to that which is good. **10** Be kindly affectioned one to another with brotherly love; in honour preferring one another; **11** Not slothful in business; fervent in spirit; serving the Lord; **12** Rejoicing in hope; patient in tribulation; continuing instant in prayer; **13** Distributing to the necessity of saints; given to hospitality. **14** Bless them which persecute you: bless, and curse not. **15** Rejoice with them that do rejoice, and weep with them that weep. **16** Be of the same mind one toward another. Mind not high things, but condescend to men of low estate. Be not wise in your own conceits. **17** Recompense to no man evil for evil. Provide things honest in the sight of all men. **18** If it be possible, as much as lieth in you, live peaceably with all men. **19** Dearly beloved, avenge not yourselves, but rather give place unto wrath: for it is written, Vengeance is mine; I will repay, saith the Lord. **20** Therefore if thine enemy hunger, feed him; if he thirst, give him drink: for in so doing thou shalt heap coals of fire on his head.

21 Be not overcome of evil, but overcome evil with good. We represent God in everything we do. Some people think well, this is my personal business that has nothing to do with God. Well I submit to you that every aspect of your life is to represent God. We do not disconnect from God to do our dirty business. Or say this is my personal life, and what I do in my personal life has nothing to do with God. This is a lie from the Kingdom of Darkness. The Kingdom of Light says Love the Lord thy God with all of your heart, mind, soul and strength. That covers every aspect of your life, even what you do in secret.

Let your yes be yes and your no be no without any manipulation.

Matthew 5:37 But let your communication be, Yea, yea; Nay, nay: for whatsoever is more than these cometh of evil.

WHEN WE HAVE TO WONDER
WHAT YOU STAND FOR!

Proverb 20:7
The just man walketh in his integrity:
his children are blessed after him.

INTEGRITY:

Your Thoughts:

Your Thoughts:

_____

_____

_____

_____

_____

_____

_____

_____

_____

_____

_____

_____

_____

_____

_____

_____

_____

_____

Your Thoughts:

Your Thoughts:

_____

_____

_____

_____

_____

_____

_____

_____

_____

_____

_____

_____

_____

_____

_____

_____

_____

FASTING

Fasting is a very vital weapon of our spiritual battle. Fasting is more than just doing without food, social media, TV or whatever you like to do. We are to spend quality quiet time with God earnestly praying, reading the word of God and worshiping him. We should seek to hear from God and desire more of him. Ask him to continue to guide, fill you with more love for him, increase your faith, love for his people and love for his word. It is not a question if you fast but when you fast. Fasting is a must!

Matthew 6:16 Moreover when ye fast, be not, as the hypocrites, of a sad countenance: for they disfigure their faces, that they may appear unto men to fast. Verily I say unto you, They have their reward. **Mark 9:22-29 22** And ofttimes it hath cast him into the fire, and into the waters, to destroy him: but if thou canst do any thing, have compassion on us, and help us. **23** Jesus said unto him, If thou canst believe, all things are possible to him that believeth. **24** And straightway the father of the child cried out, and said with tears, Lord, I believe; help thou mine unbelief. **25** When Jesus saw that the people came running together, he rebuked the foul spirit, saying unto him, Thou dumb and deaf spirit, I charge thee, come out of him, and enter no more into him. **26** And the spirit cried, and rent him sore, and came out of him: and he was as one dead; insomuch that many said, He is dead. **27** But Jesus took him by the hand, and lifted him up; and he arose. **28** And when he was come into the house, his disciples asked him privately, Why could not we cast him out? **29** And he said unto them, This kind can come forth by nothing, but by prayer and fasting.

FASTING:

Your Thoughts:

Your Thoughts:

_____

_____

_____

_____

_____

_____

_____

_____

_____

_____

_____

_____

_____

_____

_____

_____

_____

_____

Your Thoughts:

Your Thoughts:

_____

_____

_____

_____

_____

_____

_____

_____

_____

_____

_____

_____

_____

_____

_____

_____

GIVE

Luke 6:38 Give, and it shall be given unto you; good measure, pressed down, and shaken together, and running over, shall men give into your bosom. For with the same measure that ye mete withal it shall be measured to you again. If someone asks you for something and you have it to give, do not send them to someone else. That is for you to do. **James 2:15** If a brother or sister be naked, and destitute of daily food,16 And one of you say unto them, Depart in peace, be ye warmed and filled; notwithstanding ye give them not those things which are needful to the body; what doth it profit? **II Corinthians 9:7** Every man according as he purposeth in his heart, so let him give; not grudgingly, or of necessity: **for God loveth a cheerful giver. Romans 11:6** For if the first fruit be holy, the lump is also holy: and if the root be holy, so are the branches. **Matthew 6:1-4** Take heed that ye do not your alms before men, to be seen of them: otherwise ye have no reward of your Father which is in heaven. **2** Therefore when thou doest thine alms, do not sound a trumpet before thee, as the hypocrites do in the synagogues and in the streets, that they may have glory of men. Verily I say unto you, They have their reward. **3** But when thou doest alms, let not thy left hand know what thy right hand doeth: **4** That thine alms may be in secret: and thy Father which seeth in secret himself shall reward thee openly. **Matthew 6:21 21** For where your treasure is, there will your heart be also.

_____

_____

_____

_____

_____

_____

GIVE:

Your Thoughts:

Your Thoughts:

Your Thoughts:

_____

_____

_____

_____

_____

_____

_____

_____

_____

_____

_____

_____

_____

_____

_____

_____

_____

_____

_____

Your Thoughts:

WITNESS

Your feet shod with the preparation of the gospel of peace. When we open our mouths to speak to people we want them to be glad to see us coming and feel even better when we leave. We bring good tidings of Jesus, our savior of the world, not in our own knowledge or strength but in the love of Jesus Christ. Seek wisdom from God to be able to accomplish this.

I Peter 3:13-15 13 And who is he that will harm you, if ye be followers of that which is good? **14** But and if ye suffer for righteousness' sake, happy are ye: and be not afraid of their terror, neither be troubled; **15** But sanctify the Lord God in your hearts: and be ready always to give an answer to every man that asketh you a reason of the hope that is in you with meekness and fear: **Proverb 16:32** He that is slow to anger is better than the mighty, and he that ruleth his spirit than he that taketh a city. When you go to represent Jesus, keep yourself under control. Do not impose yourself over the will of others and get angry. We are excited that you are zealous to tell others but never at the expense of arguing or brawling matches. **Hebrew 12:14** Follow peace with all men, and holiness, without which no man shall see the Lord:

If Jesus was standing there would you say that?

Revelations 12:11 And they overcame him by the blood of the Lamb, and by the word of their testimony; and they loved not their lives unto the death. We overcame Satan by the blood of Jesus and by the words of our testimonies, witnessing, telling others and praising the Lord for how he brought us out. We would not stop telling others or change our testimonies of our experiences with God even if it cost us our lives.

WITNESS:

Your Thoughts:

_____

_____

_____

_____

_____

_____

_____

_____

_____

_____

_____

_____

_____

_____

_____

_____

_____

_____

Your Thoughts:

Your Thoughts:

_____
_____
_____
_____
_____
_____
_____
_____
_____
_____
_____
_____
_____
_____
_____
_____

Your Thoughts:

_____

_____

_____

_____

_____

_____

_____

_____

_____

_____

_____

_____

_____

_____

_____

_____

_____

_____

_____

OVERCOMERS

Remember warriors, Jesus has already defeated Satan. All we have to do is walk in his footsteps and have faith that all things are pos-sible.

Luke 10:19 Behold, I give unto you power to tread on serpents and scorpions, and overall the power of the enemy: and nothing shall by any means hurt you. Sometimes we sit and watch reruns of movies, football, basketball games, and boxing matches, etc. We watch with confidence no mat-ter what happens in between. We already know the outcome of who wins and who loses. "Now, you already know what I am about to say." When we are in an up close and person-al battle with a foot in the tire and the devil has his foot in the same tire, that no matter what happens in the between we have confidence in the outcome because Jesus has already defeated Satan. Understand this people of God, He knows what's best for us. We will know Jesus in the fel-lowship of His suffering. We will be tried in the fire but come out as pure gold. We all have our cross to bear. Must Jesus bear this cross alone and all the world go free? No, there is a cross for every-one and there is a cross for me. Life happens to us all but with Jesus no matter what we are victorious. Sometimes our problem is we do not like the outcome. We want to dictate to God what we think is best. He knows what is best for us because he created us **He is our Sovereign God.**

"It is just that simple, TRUST GOD."

We must put all of our heart, soul, mind and strength to Love God and His word, do not doubt but count it all joy. You think that is crazy uh? Well what about drug addicts, alcoholics, gamblers, greed, lasciviousness, murderers etc. these people lose everything for their cause and it seems that others understand that crazy.

God gave us everything when He gave His only Son Je-sus, then we must give up everything to follow Him. It is just that simple. I think sometimes we complicate it by thinking that it cannot be that simple.

He is the Potter, we are the clay, **Do not get offended by God.**

TRUST the process, we have everything to gain!

James 1:2-21 2 My brethren, count it all joy when ye fall into divers temptations; **3** Knowing this, that the trying of your faith worketh patience. **4** But let patience have her perfect work, that ye may be perfect and entire, wanting nothing. **5** If any of you lack wisdom, let him ask of God, that giveth to all men liberally, and upbraideth not; and it shall be given him. **6** But let him ask in faith, nothing wavering. For he that wavereth is like a wave of the sea driven with the wind and tossed. **7** For let not that man think that he shall receive any thing of the Lord. **8** A double minded man is unstable in all his ways. **9** Let the brother of low degree rejoice in that he is exalted: **10** But the rich, in that he is made low: because as the flower of the grass he shall pass away. **11** For the sun is no sooner risen with a burn-ing heat, but it withereth the grass, and the flower thereof falleth, and the grace of the fashion of it perisheth: so also shall the rich man fade away in his ways. **12 Blessed is the man that endureth temptation: for when he is tried, he shall receive the crown of life, which the Lord hath promised to them that love him. 13 Let no man say when he is tempted, I am tempted of God: for God cannot be tempted with evil, neither tempteth he any man: 14 But every man is tempted, when he is drawn away of his own lust, and enticed. 15 Then when lust hath conceived, it bringeth forth sin: and sin, when it is finished, bringeth forth death.**

16 Do not err, my beloved brethren. **17** Every good gift and every perfect gift is from above, and cometh down from the Father of lights, with whom is no variableness, neither shadow of turning. **18** Of his own will begat he us with the word of truth, that we should be a kind of firstfruits of his creatures. **19** Wherefore, my beloved brethren, let every man be swift to hear, slow to speak, slow to wrath: **20** For the wrath of man worketh not the righteousness of God. **21** Wherefore lay apart all filthiness and superfluity of naughtiness, and receive with meekness the engrafted word, which is able to save your souls.

My dear Brothers and Sisters, did you know sin grows (your ugly thoughts turn into ugly ways) in the Kingdom of Darkness. Just like faith grows in the Word of God (godly thought turns into godly ways) the Kingdom of Light. When we get all caught up in the pleasures of this world then it grows and grows and only God knows what we will become. Before you get to that point of self-destruction, cut it off, cut it out of your life. No matter what you have to do, break free from it!

Sin is heavy and sin is death! With the help of the Lord Jesus, in the process of time through fasting, praying, worshiping, jour-naling, singing hymns of encouragement to yourself, reading your Bible, therapy, confessing, staying away from negative people, sep-arating yourself from it kills that desire - urge.

You will not kill what you like to do. Therefore, you have to grow in faith in the Kingdom of Light until you get to the point that you hate that sin, because GOD hates sin. I never said that this road was easy. Jesus said, **Matthew 11:30 For my yoke is easy, and my burden is light.**

"We are overcomers because we choose to walk in the Kingdom of Light."

JOHN 16:33
These things I have spoken unto you, that in me ye might have peace. In the world ye shall have tribulation: but be of good cheer; I have overcome the world.

OVERCOMERS:

Your Thoughts:

_____

_____

_____

_____

_____

_____

_____

_____

_____

_____

_____

_____

_____

_____

_____

_____

_____

Your Thoughts:

Your Thoughts:

_____
_____
_____
_____
_____
_____
_____
_____
_____
_____
_____
_____
_____
_____
_____
_____
_____

Your Thoughts:

_____

_____

_____

_____

_____

_____

_____

_____

_____

_____

_____

_____

_____

_____

_____

_____

_____

_____

STUDY FOR YOURSELF

- Always take time to study and read or listen to the word of God. God's word is the map to eternal life in peace, just think about that... If you do not know how to study, there are lesson plans in your digital Bible on your phone or computer. You can also buy books with lesson plans.

2 Timothy 2:15-19 15 Study to shew thyself approved unto God, a workman that needeth not to be ashamed, rightly dividing the word of truth. **16** But shun profane and vain babblings: for they will increase unto more ungodliness. **17** And their word will eat as doth a canker: of whom is Hymenaeus and Philetus; **18** Who concerning the truth have erred, saying that the resurrection is past already; and overthrow the faith of some. **19** Nevertheless the foundation of God standeth sure, having this seal, The Lord knoweth them that are his. And, let every one that nameth the name of Christ depart from iniquity. We must be fully persuaded and confident in our minds that the plan of salvation through Jesus Christ is the one and only true gospel to get to heaven. Jesus is our only savior, mediator, Lord of Lords and King of Kings.

EPHESIANS 4:4-6
There is one body, and one Spirit, even as ye are called in one hope of your calling;
5 One Lord, one faith, one baptism,
6 One God and Father of all, who is above all, and through all, and in you all.

_____

_____

_____

_____

_____

STUDY FOR YOURSELF:

Your Thoughts:

_____
_____
_____
_____
_____
_____
_____
_____
_____
_____
_____
_____
_____
_____
_____
_____
_____
_____

Your Thoughts:

Your Thoughts:

_____

_____

_____

_____

_____

_____

_____

_____

_____

_____

_____

_____

_____

_____

_____

_____

_____

Your Thoughts:

_____

_____

_____

_____

_____

_____

_____

_____

_____

_____

_____

_____

_____

_____

_____

_____

_____

_____

NOTES

NOTES

NOTES

NOTES

Prayer:

Oh, Father in heaven teach me how to be aware of Your
ever-presence in my life. Open my spiritual eyes to see the tricks the devil
tries to deceive me with in my thoughts. May my heart's desire always be
to please You in the ultimate outcome of every situation. I know that your
grace is sufficient and you give us new mercies every morning. I pray that I
take advantage of everyday to let your light shine so that others see my good
works and glorify the Father which is in heaven.

In Jesus Mighty Name Amen!

Philippians 2:12

10 That at the name of Jesus every knee should bow, of things in heaven, and things in earth, and things under the earth; 11 And that every tongue should confess that Jesus Christ is Lord, to the glory of God the Father.
12 Wherefore, my beloved, as ye have always obeyed, not as in my presence only, but now much more in my absence,

work out your own salvation with fear and trembling.

Mary Caldwell Evans

REFERENCE

The Holy Bible - King James Version (KJV)

www.ingramcontent.com/pod-product-compliance
Lightning Source LLC
Chambersburg PA
CBHW051319120626
46547CB00015B/2303